Th
GENESIS
Of Manhood

THE HEROIC MAN'S JOURNEY

Contents

Preface

God created a man and he was marvelous. The gift of being made in God's image provided him with amazing potential; he was given the opportunity to experience a walk with God so personal it is hard to even imagine it. *The Genesis of Manhood* reminds us of the original plan God had for us, as men. God designed us with the specific plan that we would communicate with Him, and with others; communication is essential to establishing intimacy within our relationships. Unfortunately, when man made the choice to sin, the Garden's ideal environment quickly crumbled. God's truth and His standards were exchanged for lies and an attitude of compromise. In our present day, life can be harsh, our relationship with God is distant, and the concept of establishing healthy relationships is challenging. In many ways, life has become negatively-focused, and the introduction of sin to the world brought catastrophic and devastating consequences.

God has not given up on us. He wants to restore us to a miraculous state. Manhood is indeed a noble quest. When a man fulfills his potential by utilizing God's strength and guidance, his experience is very different from what we see the males around us experiencing. To achieve manhood, a male must have the courage and motivation to look at the ways sin hinders his life; he must seek Jesus Christ's transforming power, and apply God's promises and purpose to every area of his life. Through the Holy Spirit's intervention in his life, a man can humbly step up and fully utilize the image of God within him, as he learns to master the complexity of what he was created to be.

Amazing technology is available to you, but if you don't read the directions, you will limit yourself by only utilizing a fraction of its complex potential. So too, many males have chosen a life of passive indifference. Boredom, violence, isolation and aimlessness abound within the males in our world, as our prisons are full, our churches are becoming weaker, and our families are destroyed. Manhood is not automatically achieved at a certain age, nor does it happen by accident. A male needs to seek manhood, and along with his band of brothers, look at what he has lost because, through Jesus, it can be found.

At Knights of the 21st Century, we do not just talk about what males should do; we create an environment where men can build relationships and challenge each other. (Hebrews 10:24) Through conversations about what is really happening in our lives, we can give and receive the support that encourages the positive changes God wants for our lives. Male passivity is transformed and we are motivated to walk with Jesus daily and reflect God's essence in all that we do. As men, our collective faith mobilizes us to be more God-like at home, to intervene with actions that provide healing in an often hostile world and to build up God's church. Popular ridicule is set aside as God's transforming message becomes clear.

The Genesis of Manhood is a 6-lesson DVD that teaches men about the plan God originally had in mind for their manhood. God is not finished with us. Despite the ugly consequences of sin, we can be restored and fulfill God's original intention through our relationship with the Ultimate Man, Jesus Christ. As children of God, our nobility will be challenged. The lies that have become part of our culture have been added to the lies we tell ourselves and the lies that males express. Our environment competes with our soul's desire to discover and follow God's plan for our lives. Personality struggles which disrupt our satisfaction with life and harm our relationships can be healed. God wants to restore the manhood He designed for us.

We will consider what happens when a manly leader takes what Jesus Christ offers at face value and with great faith, demonstrates the life-changing miracles that can be experienced. The miraculous that occurs within your own changed life can extend to others as your family begins to experience who you are, as a representative of God's love in their lives.

God wants to do the same for you. Learning how to walk with Him daily through the challenges of life is a great place to begin. It's time to stop being passive and say with passion – Let's get it done with God! As a group of men, we do not want to leave any man behind. Men often have ambivalence about sharing within a group setting because it is easier to avoid some areas of life than talk about them. Establishing the practice of meeting together regularly for comradeship, encouragement and learning benefits you, and as your relationship skills grow, it can become something you really look forward to.

Don't lose the momentum you create with your team or squander your investment of time and energy. When you have completed *The Genesis of Manhood*, find other ways to continue your quest, as a team, for becoming the men God wants you to be. Because of Christ, the church's important message is shared, and its mission to see lives positively changed is established – all of which builds up the body of Christ. This is one of the chief purposes of manhood. The culture is hurting. We need men who are willing to mobilize and demonstrate God's way to the world. We need men who will defend their families. We need men to win the spiritual war in our world. (Ephesians 6:12)

You can make a difference which will erase the sense of defeat we all talk about and the worry we have about our children's future, and turn it into a victory that blesses all of us. I encourage you to follow this in-depth introduction to the plan God has for our manhood with the 24-lesson DVD called *SQUIRE: THE TRAINING OF THE KNIGHT*. This program will provide an in-depth focus on even more aspects of your manhood walk, as you learn to apply Jesus to the parts of yourself you are yet to discover. With God's assistance, you will be challenged to fulfill His specific purpose for your life, and demonstrate His original design which began at the genesis of manhood.

Lesson 1
<u>God's Two Plans</u>

I. God was there in the beginning. He is the motivating force for all that is.

   A. How God created life is less significant than the purpose He had for creating it. (Genesis 1:1)

   B. God used His likeness (or image) as a model for creating man. (Genesis 1:27)

   C. God created man with a purposeful expectation of forming a _relationship_ with him; within this relationship, He created ways that communication and interaction could occur between them. (Genesis 1:28)

   D. When God created man, He assigned him a specific job which would require effort (work). (Genesis 2:15)

God assigned man to:

   1. Rule over, manage and take care of the environment. (Genesis 1:28)

   2. Create a family to help him deal with what is happening in the world (reality). (Genesis 2:24)

3. Put effort into understanding the details of life by:

- Being fully aware of what is happening around him.

- Increasing his ability to use words to explain what he experiences, so that he can process what is going on around him and discuss it with others. (Genesis 2:19)

- Accepting that "all that is" – is a __Gift__ from God. (Genesis 1:29-30)

E. God expects a man to:

1. Remember what God has told him regarding his limitations. (Genesis 2:16-17)

2. Develop supportive relationships with others who are different from him because life is too challenging to do alone. (Genesis 2:18)

3. Accept himself, regardless of the point in life he is at. (Genesis 2:25)

4. Communicate with Him daily. (Genesis 3:8)

II. Man chose to ignore God's initial plan for relational intimacy by trying to become as "smart" as God, which brought about the destructive force God calls sin. (Genesis 3:5)

This caused man to:

A. Harm himself.

B. Behave negatively toward others.

C. Create a challenging and hostile environment.

D. Have the need for a Savior.

III. Although sin dramatically changed life for humankind over the ages, God:

A. Continues to be the omnipotent spiritual force behind what each of us experiences in everyday life.

B. Made us in His image. This gift provides us with characteristics which no other form of life possesses.

1. As a result of the spiritual deadness of the human spirit, we need God to resurrect our spirits.

2. As immature males, when we choose to behave in primitive ways, we deny the nobility we, as men, were given when God created us. (Children of God status – Galatians 3:26)

3. We are called to act as God's representatives in the lives of others. (Galatians 2:20)

C. Gave each of us a specific job (a purpose) which includes:

1. Mastering our personal environments by changing what we can, _Adusting_ to what we can't change and taking care of our world for our children. (Philippians 4:11)

2. Engaging with others in relationally positive ways. (John 13:34-35)

3. Learning to accept and understand the details that are required in order to live life well.

   • What are God's expectations for our lives, as written in the Bible? (2 Timothy 3:16)

   • What are the effects of the fall of man? With God's help, how can a man live a victorious life? (1 Corinthians 15:55-57)

   • Assign words to the various processes, events, experiences and aspects of our lives so that we can responsibly choose how to integrate God into these areas. (Colossians 3:17)

4. Accepting that His guidance is a gift to us, even when we are distressed by what is happening in our lives. (Psalm 32:8)

D. Expects a man to:

1. Develop a relationship with Him by accepting what Jesus Christ has done for him. (John 1:12)

2. Remember what He has told him about the actions that hinder their relationship with each other. (John 17:15-16)

3. Engage in supportive relationships with his family and friends. (1 Peter 3:8)

4. Walk with Him on a daily basis; represent Him in his love for others; integrate His will into each aspect of his life. (1 Thessalonians 5:17)

5. Follow His plan two.

Group Discussion: Share your answers with your group.

1. Briefly talk about your week, sharing the highlights or the concerns you may have.

2. Share a thought or an idea that stood out to you from this lesson.

3. What would you like to get out of your time with this group of men?

4. What does being made "in the likeness of God" mean to you? (Genesis 5:1)

5. Genesis 2:18 states: "The LORD God said, 'It is not good for man to be alone.'" What do you think this Bible verse means?

6. Discuss the pros and cons of your personal environment. How are you affected by it, either positively or negatively?

7. Review the expectations of man in Section I (D); which do you believe God has called you to do?

8. Matthew 7:13-14 states: "'Enter God's kingdom through the narrow gate. The gate is large and the road is wide that lead to death and hell. Many people go that way. But the gate is small and the road is narrow that lead to life. Only a few people find it.'" How do these Bible verses apply to your manhood journey?

Lesson 2
<u>Unhelpful Consequences</u>

There are negative consequences when a man chooses to dismiss God's original plan.

I. There are external consequences that work against a man's ability to follow God's call for his life. (John 5:5-8) These consequences impact a man's life in the following ways:

   A. Life is difficult; we are each challenged by hardship and loss. The individual losses that we experience require us to:

      1. Leave our _____ zones. (Genesis 37:19-26)

      2. Say goodbye to those we love. (John 11:31-36)

      3. Adjust to negative circumstances which are often unexpected. (1 Corinthians 10:13)

   B. We add to our difficulties when we make unwise choices.

      1. In each troublesome situation, there is one common denominator – _____. (Romans 3:23)

      2. We struggle repeatedly with whether to follow God or ourselves. (Luke 9:23)

3. We form relationships with people who have destructive agendas and influence us negatively. (Genesis 4:2-8)

   Because of this, we must:

   - Protect ourselves and our families from those who want to harm us. (John 7:19)

   - Recognize the need to set boundaries with those we love because of our imperfections. (Mark 8:33)

   - Be sensitive to the ways that peer pressure affects us. (2 Corinthians 6:14)

   - Understand the ways that our individual struggles are intensified by the actions of others. (Proverbs 7:18-21)

   - Choose to forgive "those who sin against us"; this allows us not to be held hostage by what they do and say. (Matthew 6:12)

   - Learn to confront our brothers; this will help them become the men God designed them to be. (Proverbs 27:17)

C. In the Garden before the fall of man, man did not know everything, but what he did know was the truth. As the result of his choice to sin, a world of lies was created. (John 8:44)

Man has created the following lies:

1. Lie – Sin is seen as a list of specific actions, instead of a pervasive negative force that affects everyone.

2. Lie – A man's personal wealth is measured by his money and possessions, not by the quality of his relationships.

3. Lie – Men are simplistic, sexually-oriented and aggressive; they do not need to expect much of themselves.

4. Lie – The best sex is not based on a committed love for one person, but on youth, variety, intense lust and a specific sexual image.

5. Lie – People are valued at different levels, as status and power takes precedence.

6. Lie – People who are like you are more trustworthy than those who are different from you.

7. Lie – That which is easily seen is more important than what is not seen (i.e., values, spirituality). (2 Corinthians 4:18)

8. Lie – Faith can only be experienced by someone who is a Christian.

9. Lie – The way and the means that a goal is achieved doesn't matter; it needs to be done any way, any how.

10. Lie – Truth is less important than doing whatever is needed in the moment.

11. Lie – "What's in it for me" outweighs what the other person needs. (Self-centered culture)

II. The environment looks forward to the time when we, as men, will be different. "Everything God created looks forward to the time when his children will appear in their full and final glory." (Romans 8:19) (The word "forest" is used to describe the environment which surrounds each man.)

III. As a result of the pressure that sin has caused, the environment (forest) groans, like the creaking of a ship, because the world was not designed for this. "We know that all that God created has been groaning. It is in pain as if it were giving birth to a child. The created world continues to groan even now." (Romans 8:22)

IV. As men, there are more internal consequences for our sin than eternal damnation. (2 Peter 2:9)

A. The Bible describes the consequences of sin with the phrase, "For the wages of sin *is* death." (Romans 6:23, NKJV) The presence of sin causes death at multiple levels, both within the forest and within ourselves.

B. Like the forest, we also groan because of the pressure created by carrying sin's consequences in our lives. "And that's not all. We have the Holy Spirit as the promise of future blessing. But we also groan inside ourselves as we look forward to the time when God will adopt us as full members of his family. Then he will give us everything he has for us. He will raise our bodies and give glory to them." (Romans 8:23)

C. Sin not only separates us from God; it keeps us from becoming the men He originally designed us to be.

   1. The presence of sin in our lives makes it hard for us to recognize and develop our potential.

   2. Sin makes it difficult for us to love others in Godly ways.

   3. Our ethics and our values are often put aside for other negatively-focused behaviors.

D. God not only wants a relationship with us for eternity, He also wants a relationship with us that is part of our everyday lives, which allows Him to help us overcome the many ways that sin limits our manhood.

Group Discussion: Share your answers with your group.

1. Briefly talk about your week, sharing the highlights or the concerns you may have. You may also want to give an update on what you shared last week.

2. Share a thought or an idea that stood out to you from this lesson.

3. Share a personal issue which challenges you and makes your life more difficult.

4. Discuss your reaction to the statement in Section I (B-1): In each troublesome situation there is one common denominator – US.

5. In which areas of life are you the most concerned about protecting your family from threats?

6. Review the list of lies in Section I (C); select one of the lies and discuss how it affects your life.

7. Psalm 141:4 states: "Don't let my heart be drawn to what is evil. Don't let me join men who do evil. They don't do what is right. Don't let me join them and eat their fancy food." How does this Bible verse apply to your manhood journey?

Lesson 3
Human Tragedy

By choosing to sin, Adam nuked God's original plan for mankind and his environment. The radiating effects of the sins of mankind on the forest are often denied, underestimated or culturally redefined. Individually, we each carry the cumulative effects of the destructive influences of sin within us.

A. The lies that are told within the forest support the lies that we tell ourselves, some of which are included in the following:

1. Lie – Who one is and what one does on a daily basis is irrelevant to any supreme being. We think we can hide from God. (Hebrews 4:13; Jeremiah 23:24)

2. Lie – We do not need to live up to what we say; it is neither an obligation nor a promise which we are expected to keep. (1 John 2:5; Matthew 5:37)

3. Lie – If it feels good, do it. (Hebrews 11:4-26)

4. Lie – It is not my responsibility to show interest in how others are doing. I have no social obligations to the people around me. Other people's issues are not my problem. (1 John 4:7)

5. Lie – I am a victim to the circumstances that I am in; it's not my fault.

6. Lie – If just one thing would happen the way I want it to, life would be good.

7. Lie – The way that other people perceive me is what really matters.

8. Lie – We are right about most things. (The truth is, we need to have a healthy self-skepticism.)

9. Lie – If I work hard enough, I can make other people change. If other people change, my life will be fine.

10. Lie – Life is either completely good or completely bad.

11. Lie – Doing "it" this one time won't hurt. (The truth is, if it hurts God, or someone we love, or ourselves, it does hurt.)

B. Some of the lies that we tell ourselves are connected to our male biology, as a result of the fall of man.

1. Lie – Might makes right. The male tendency to want to dominate is expressed freely.

   • Real personal power is about _____ strength, not physical strength.

   • Power can be a corrupting force.

2. As a man, I am tough; I don't need relationships.

- Truth is like the runner who needs others to push him to be his best; we need others who encourage us and push us toward truth, which helps us to be our best.

- The predators of life attack us most when we are alone.

- In His life, Jesus demonstrated the importance of developing supportive relationships.

3. Lie – Feelings are for women. As a man, I should deny what I am feeling.

- I am not aware of my feelings or how to express them. I fail to recognize how my feelings fit into the bigger picture of who I am.

- God created me to have feelings; feelings help me communicate His message of love to others.

- Much of what I need to become aware of in life is first sensed at a feeling (or intuition) level.

- God is passionate toward me. I need to experience my passion for Him.

4. Lie – If I don't do it, someone else will.

- God has blessed you with an assignment for which He has given you unique skills and gifts; the completion of His assignment will honor Him.

- Giving in to your male tendency to be passive limits God's ability to help you become the man He designed you to be.

- The forest is harmed by my choice not to follow God's call to make a difference in the forest.

5. Lie – Someday, I will do that. (Proverbs 27:1; James 4:14; Mark 13:32-33)

   - My decision to put off the choices that are needed, in order to become the man God wants me to be, causes my priorities to be misaligned.

   - Waiting creates boredom which is often followed by other negative choices.

6. Lie – Women are here to take care of me.

   - I am surprised when my wife, who I want to treat me like my mother did, is not interested in being romantic.

   - I fail to love her for who she is; instead, I focus on what she does for me.

   - I fail to lead sacrificially, "as Christ led the church." (Ephesians 5:25)

7. Lie – Sexual release is one of the most important daily experiences of a man's life.
   (1 Thessalonians 4:3-5)

- Despite the power of the testosterone hormone, you are more than your _____.

- Men destroy their ability to experience _____ intimacy because of their obsession with sex.

C. When the lies found in the forest are combined with the lies that humans tell themselves and the lies commonly told by males, a destructive force is created that negatively influences our lives and our world.

1. Separation from God is devastating, from the perspective of life on earth, as well as from an eternal perspective.

2. God must reach down to us and send us a Savior; without Him as our Savior, we will remain eternally divorced from Him.

3. Life on earth has been altered as the Garden of Eden lifestyle, which Adam initially enjoyed, has been changed.

4. Our bodies are different, as aging and death become inevitable.

5. Our human spirits are dead. Unless our spirit is resurrected (or reborn) through a relationship with Jesus Christ, our communication with a Holy God is limited. (John 3:3)

6. After the fall, human personalities were changed as anger, anxiety, depression, denial, distress, blame, callousness, narcissism, domination, somatization and other forms of imbalance are part of the human experience.

Group Discussion: Share your answers with your group.

1. Briefly talk about your week, sharing the highlights or the concerns you may have. You may also want to give an update on what you shared last week.

2. Share a thought or an idea that stood out to you from this lesson.

3. Review the list of common lies described in Section A; identify one lie that you struggle with. How do you deal with this lie in your life? How would you like to change your approach to this area of your life?

4. Review the list of common lies described in Section B; identify one lie that you struggle with. How do you deal with this lie in your life? How would you like to change your approach to this area of your life?

5. Review the personality characteristics in Section C (6). Describe a time in your life when you struggled with any of the following issues: anger, anxiety, depression, denial, distress, blame, callousness, narcissism, domination, somatization or other forms of imbalance.

6. If God has blessed you by giving you an assignment and the gifts that can help you accomplish it, tell the group what you believe God has called you to do.

7. John 8:44 states: "You belong to your father, the devil. You want to obey your father's wishes. 'From the beginning, the devil was a murderer. He has never obeyed the truth. There is no truth in him. When he lies, he speaks his natural language. He does this because he is a liar. He is the father of lies.'" How does this Bible verse apply to your manhood journey?

Lesson 4
<u>Fulfilling God's Plan</u>

I. It is God's desire that you believe in Jesus Christ and accept Him as your Lord and Savior. This allows:

A. Your human spirit to be resurrected, enabling you to communicate with Him. (John 3:8)

B. You to experience His forgiveness; His forgiveness begins to relieve the distress caused by the human tragedy. (1 John 1:9)

C. You to receive His guidance; God wants to be a positive force in your life and help you to develop your full potential. (Proverbs 3:5-6)

D. You to feel His presence, as you make pragmatic choices regarding how to live life.

E. You to fully engage with your original design, as you integrate Him into the complex areas of your life.

F. You to utilize His power to avoid future self-destructive choices.

G. You to fulfill His purpose in your life by your unique representation of _____ in all of your relationships.

H. You to share His message of love and salvation with others and inspire them to make a similar spiritual choice. (Matthew 28:19-20)

II. God wants us to apply His perspective and influence to every aspect of our lives. In order to do His will:

A. Our bodies should be viewed as His temple; our bodies should not be defiled, but honored.

B. We should base our personal decisions on what we learn from the Bible. "Never stop reading this Scroll of the Law. Day and night you must think about what it says. Make sure you do everything that is written in it. Then things will go well with you. And you will have great success." (Joshua 1:8)

C. We need to communicate regularly with Him through prayer. "Look to the LORD and to his strength. Always look to him." (1 Chronicles 16:11)

D. We need to stay in tune with God's will; when we do, He will give us what we want. "Find your delight in the LORD. Then he will give you everything your heart really wants." (Psalm 37:4)

E. We need to interact regularly with our Christian brothers; this will help us become more Christ-like. "As iron sharpens iron, so one person sharpens another." (Proverbs 27:17)

III. We need to be aware of our personality traits and make the changes which allow God to be seen in everything we do. We have negative personality tendencies which we must ask God to help us with. Place a check mark (✓) beside each tendency that is a struggle for you:

___A. Our tendency to _____ others, which is a way to avoid taking responsibility for our choices.

___B. Our self-focused nature which causes us to be insensitive to the needs of others.

___C. Our use of behaviors and substances (food, drugs, alcohol, work, sex) to avoid feeling our emotions and facing reality.

___D. Our anger, when it is expressed in sinful ways. (Ephesians 4:26)

   ___1. Expressing ourselves with words or moods that are threatening, dominating, explosive or harsh.

   ___2. Expressing our anger and hurt in indirect ways (passive aggressive).

___E. The ways we misuse our bodies when we internalize the stress of the unresolved issues in our lives can make us physically sick.

___F. Our choice to become dramatic, as a way of avoiding the hard work that is required by facing reality, developing a plan and executing it.

___G. Our choice to distrust others instead of doing the hard work of getting to know them.

___H. Choosing to hang onto resentment from our past and not forgiving those who hurt us.

___I. Our anxiety over what life may bring us in the future, which allows fear to rule our choices.

___J. Our choice to deny what is going on around us, which allows us to create a fantasy that we are not part of the problem and everything will be okay.

___K. Our choice to be so concerned about the details that we fail to see the big picture.

___L. Our choice not to grieve and not to work through our sadness by expecting others to fix us.

___M. Allowing our self-criticism to get so loud that we fail to try.

___N. Our failure to develop basic social skills which inhibits our ability to relate to others in ways that help them feel loved.

___O. Feeling so worthless and debilitated by guilt that we ignore the gifts God has given to us which are needed to develop our potential and use it for His service. (This inhibits us from feeling the true grace of God through the death of His Son, Jesus, causing us to feel like we must martyr ourselves.)

___P. Our choice to give ourselves the benefit of the doubt while expecting others to be punished, instead of granting them the same understanding that we give ourselves.

___Q. Our lack of conscience, which makes it easy for us to harm others in order to get something we want.

___R. Our prejudice, which encourages us to diminish or demean those who are different from us.

___S. Our inconsistent practice of the values we claim to espouse.

___T. Our choice to hide our true feelings and pretend to be someone other than who we are, which causes us not to be authentic.

___U. Our failure to live life in a structured or organized way which fosters an identity that is defined as chaotic.

___V. Using our intellect to avoid or deny our underlying feelings.

___W. In order to prove something to ourselves, we are driven by our work, like Martha (Luke 10:38-42); this causes us to miss the joy of having God present in our lives.

___X. Our choice not to act on the negative experiences from our past which ultimately leads to our failure to resolve the ways they impact our lives and our relationships. (Exodus 25)

___Y. Saying what we feel before we think about how to express these feelings in ways that can be heard by others. (Ephesians 4:15)

___Z. Our attempt to live our lives through others; when we do this, we establish a dependent lifestyle which inhibits our ability to develop our own identify with God.

IV. We experience the contradiction between what God has called us for and who we are. (Romans 7:24-25)

Some people:

A. Are overwhelmed with guilt.

B. Are less concerned about their sin, because they know they can rely on God's grace and forgiveness. (Romans 6:1)

C. Give up any hope of positive change regarding their personality traits in their earthly life.

D. Start the journey of becoming who God called them to be.

Group Discussion: Share your answers with your group.

1. Briefly talk about your week, sharing the highlights or the concerns you may have. You may also want to give an update on what you shared last week.

2. Share a thought or an idea that stood out to you from this lesson.

3. Review the benefits described in Section I; select one that you appreciate, as a result of your belief in Jesus Christ.

4. Is it easy or hard for you to take care of yourself physically? Remember, to be your best, you must be willing to see a doctor and a dentist regularly!

5. Review the list of negative personality tendencies you checked off in Section III; identify the one that you struggle with the most and would like to improve.

6. Psalm 142:1-2 states: "I call out to the LORD. I pray to him for his favor. I pour out my problem to him. I tell him about my trouble." How do these Bible verses apply to your manhood journey?

Lesson 5
<u>The Restoration</u>

I. At times, the realization of our human tragedy creates such distress that we try to defend ourselves, so as not to feel totally insignificant. God wants us to be aware of the various ways that sin has impacted us, as humans.

   A. People deny their human tragedy by failing to recognize their spiritual nature and the implications of their sin.

      1. The problems (lies) that we see around us – just are; they do not have an underlying spiritual cause.

      2. We use the promise of God's grace to blind ourselves from our need of God's redemption.

      3. When we live a life that is filled with addictive choices, rigid patterns or disinterest, our human spirit is _____ by something other than what God originally designed it for.

   B. People redefine God in order to attempt to fix their sin themselves. (Religious)

      1. People believe in a system of good works which is meant to attain God's favor in some unidentified way.

2. People develop a specific list of "shoulds" to distract themselves from what is happening in many areas of their daily lives.

3. People limit their awareness of their present sinful state by ignoring it and by not engaging in honest self-assessment. In church, they pretend they are more spiritually focused than they truly are.

C. People deny God's existence (atheistic position) and by doing so, make their sin and its spiritual consequences irrelevant.

D. People accept that a relationship with God is necessary and start exploring how to establish a relationship with Jesus Christ. (Justification)

1. As a result of a daily walk with Jesus, God shows them how to live a positive life now. (Sanctification)

2. Accepting Jesus as their Savior changes their eternal destination.

3. Following God's guidance improves their day-to-day life on earth.

4. Their spiritual rebirth helps them experience a fully satisfying life.

5. Jesus empowers them to develop their full potential.

6. You will fulfill God's call for your life if you believe in Jesus and ask Him to be your Lord.

II. In order for a man to be what God wants him to be, he must understand the various ways that sin _____ affects him. (Galatians 6:7-8)

A. He cannot apply God's principles to the areas of his life that he is not tuned into. (Proverbs 6:27-29)

B. When a man is growing spiritually, there are two interdependent themes which happen repeatedly. (2 Corinthians 4:16-18)

1. He is increasingly more aware of God's presence in everything he does which increases the ways he relies on God's empowerment to live his life. (1 Chronicles 29:13-14)

2. He examines his life for the ways that his walk with God is hindered. By looking at the areas and situations in which he creates spiritual barriers, it is easier for him to feel God's active involvement in each facet of his life. (1 Timothy 1:5-6)

3. He needs God's help to see and feel His presence and to recognize the barriers he creates in his relationship with Him. (Psalm 7:14-15)

- This requires a regular time of quiet reflection, during which he allows God to speak while he listens. (Psalm 46:10)

- There are Bible stories which portray man's relationship with God over time. (Hebrews 11:1-10)

- For this to happen, he must be honest with himself regarding his true nature. (Jeremiah 17:10)

- It emphasizes an attitude of humility (Ephesians 4:2), as he recognizes his imperfections and his reliance on God's willingness to forgive him.

- It increases his tolerance of others, who also have imperfections. (Matthew 6:14-15)

- It creates a need for supportive relationships (Hebrews 10:25) with other men who:

  ◇ Encourage him not to give up. (1 Thessalonians 5:11)

  ◇ Provide him with opportunities for growth. (1 John 3:16-18)

  ◇ Confront his character defects. (Proverbs 27:17)

III. Becoming more Christ-like requires you to become a man, which means leaving your childish (male) ways behind. (1 Corinthians 13:11)

A. You must pursue strategies which will help you _____ your wounds from the past and move on to a life of victory by:
(Ephesians 4:22-23)

   1. Forgiving yourself for your past mistakes, as God has forgiven you.

   2. Focusing on the good you have received from your parents and building on it.

   3. Learning to differentiate between wise and unwise choices and not repeating the mistakes your mom and dad made. (Exodus 20:5)

   4. Resolving the relationship rejections that you have experienced.

   5. Resolving the problematic issues in your life so that they are not passed on to the next generation. (Refer to Abraham and Isaac's treatment of their wives.)

B. You must develop all of your potential and utilize it for the pursuit of manhood. (1 Corinthians 12:7)

C. You must seek God's guidance constantly. (Deuteronomy 4:29)

D. You must recognize your complexity and put effort into understanding your God-given design. (Psalm 139:14)

E. You must learn that when you isolate yourself, you make yourself vulnerable to despair; instead, seek relationships which support your manhood journey. (Luke 6:38)

F. You must forgive others to prevent your serenity from being held hostage by their negative acts. (Ephesians 4:31-32)

G. You must portray a toughness of character and maintain your commitment to your values, no matter what the cost is. (Hebrews 10:36)

H. You must apply God's gifts to your life which will, in turn, enhance your relationships. (Leviticus 25:35)

I. You must confess your sins to God and accept His forgiveness. (1 John 1:9)

J. You must lead in a self-sacrificial manner, as Christ led the church. (Ephesians 5:25)

IV. To be the strongest man you can be, you must meet regularly with other men. (Hebrews 10:25)

A. Life is challenging and gives us many reasons to quit. (Jeremiah 17:7-8)

B. God wants you to serve other men, which then enables them to serve others. (Matthew 5:19)

C. You need to reach out to others who do not know God. (Matthew 28:19-20)

Group Discussion: Share your answers with your group.

1. Briefly talk about your week, sharing the highlights or the concerns you may have. You may also want to give an update on what you shared last week.

2. Share a thought or an idea that stood out to you from this lesson.

3. Is it more difficult for you to recognize God's presence in everything you do, or to be aware of the barriers you use to separate yourself from Him? Why?

4. Discuss whether it is easy or difficult for you to display each of the following manly characteristics: honesty, humility, tolerance and creating supportive relationships.

5. Identify a difficult issue or a wound from your past that you need to resolve in order to feel victorious.

6. In which areas of your life are you asking God for His guidance?

7. Identify a person from your past who hurt you. How did you practice the act of forgiveness in this situation?

8. Psalm 142:5 states: "Lord, I cry out to you. I say, 'You are my place of safety. You are everything I need in this life.'" How does this Bible verse apply to your manhood journey?

Lesson 6
The Call

I. Lesson Review

   1. God had a plan and a purpose for men in the garden that included communication with Him.

   2. Men chose to sin. As a result of sin, a pervasive human tragedy occurred.

   3. There are many unhelpful consequences that are the result of sin, one of which is the negative personality attributes that men have as part of their character.

   4. The fulfillment of God's new plan requires us to establish a relationship with Jesus and apply His strength to our character defects.

   5. Restoration is a process that requires us to be aware of God's presence; we must also recognize the barriers that we have created between ourselves and God. As Godly men, we must learn to put childish behaviors and choices behind.

II. In Matthew 8:5-13, there is a brief story about Jesus meeting a Roman commander, who was a man's man.

   A. He is caring, despite the other man's status.

   B. Despite the power he had, he realized it was not enough to deal with all of life's needs.

C. He didn't just identify a problem – he expended his energy to get it fixed.

D. He kept his past accomplishments in perspective because he knew that compared to Jesus, he was unworthy.

E. He had a _____ view of his authority and accepted that Jesus was the true authority.

F. He was able to understand more than those who had been religiously trained.

G. He was celebrated by Jesus because he knew how to apply his faith.

H. He got the results he asked for.

I. We need to be like this Roman commander and make a choice about who the authority is in our lives. In our Knights program, we say that God has called us to be knights of this 21st century; we are called to _____ our King, Jesus.

III. God, as the Ultimate Authority, has called you for a purpose which He designed only for you.

A. You have great value; your value is not simply based on His love; it is also because of the contributions you can make to the lives of others, as His representative on earth.

1. This is a very high calling because it honors God.

2. Only you are the unique person who is someone's son, brother, husband, father, grandfather or friend.

3. Your role in the lives of others creates an opportunity for them to hear God's message through you.

4. You have unique skills which can be utilized to enhance the lives of others, whether you have the ability to fix cars, give positive advice, share a word of encouragement or pray. Regardless of what your unique, God-given skill is, you are necessary.

5. The church needs you to not only contribute financially, but more importantly, it needs you to contribute physically and spiritually because this is how you can help move its mission forward.

6. The world is filled with desperate people who are spiritually lost, people who need to hear about your faith in Jesus, and see Him reflected in your actions and words. (James 1:22)

B. When you look around the world (forest), there is a lot to complain about.

1. You keep saying, "It can't get worse," and then it does.

2. You are angry about the violence that is occurring in the world.

3. You see people you love who are being hurt.

4. You are worried about the lack of values in the world and where it is taking us.

5. You want to be more like God, which means not going along with the crowd.

C. The choice is fairly stark! Einstein defined insanity as doing the same thing over and over again, expecting a different result.

1. Choice 1: You can ignore God's call for your life; you can stay in your comfort zone; you can continue to follow the patterns of the past. But, you will:

   • Remain bored.

   • Lose the opportunity to use the challenges of life to develop yourself.

   • Not honor God by fulfilling the purpose He has designed for you.

   • Be letting the problems around you compound as you wait.

   • Fail to support your band of brothers who recognize the spiritual war that we are in.

   • Miss the adventure of experiencing how a fully functioning man of God feels and acts.

- Not help those in need by creating positive change in our world.

2. Choice 2: You can listen to God, and step out as a man by:

   - Fully developing your relationship with God.

   - Applying what God teaches to each aspect of your life, including your personality style.

   - Sharing your gifts willingly with others.

   - Joining a group of men who are _____ to each other's well-being, growth and spiritual journey.

   - Making a difference in the area of the forest where God has placed you.

   - Preparing yourself for the challenges ahead.

IV. A man of God:

A. Recognizes the complexity of God's design and puts effort into understanding himself. (Psalm 139:14)

B. Understands that when he is isolated, he is vulnerable; these are the times when he is most likely to despair or be attacked; he knows he must seek relationships which support his manhood journey. (Luke 6:38)

C. Forgives others; when he forgives, his serenity is not held hostage by the negative acts of others. (Ephesians 4:31-32)

D. Portrays a toughness of character which demonstrates his ongoing commitment to his values, no matter what the cost is. (Hebrews 10:36)

E. Applies all of God's gifts to the enhancement of his relationships. (Leviticus 25:35)

F. Confesses his sin to God and accepts His forgiveness. (1 John 1:9)

G. Leads in a self-sacrificial manner, as Christ led the church. (Ephesians 5:25)

V. As a man of God, you need to overcome the male tendency to isolate yourself; your family, your church and your community needs you to join an army that can make our world a better place.

A. Life requires a man to be pro-active; set a time to meet, plan an agenda that is designed to help you and other men grow; leave no man behind.

B. Don't stop the positive relational momentum that you have established by completing *The Genesis of Manhood*; keep the progress toward manhood going!

C. If manhood is not actively maintained, it will be gradually lost.

D. Consider the next program in our Knights of the 21ˢᵗ Century manhood series, THE HEROIC MAN'S JOURNEY, which begins with SQUIRE: THE TRAINING OF THE KNIGHT.

You will:

1. Learn to understand the complexity of God's design, individualized for you, in simpler terms.

2. Discover how you are affected by your instincts.

3. Explore the importance and function of your core and how it can help you become all you were created to be.

4. Develop positive relational skills.

5. Learn how to apply what God teaches to many areas of your life, often in new ways.

6. Start utilizing the "15 Principles of Manhood" (**http://bit.ly/principlesofmanhood** or **http://bit.ly/1ueLjr7**) to guide your life.

7. Become a better follower of Christ, which will help you become a better husband, father and friend.

Group Discussion: Share your answers with your group.

1. Briefly talk about your week, sharing the highlights or the concerns you may have. You may also want to give an update on what you shared last week.

2. Share a thought or an idea that stood out to you from this lesson.

3. Review the manhood principles the Roman commander demonstrated (Section II); select one of the principles and explain how it is manly. How can you apply this principle to your life?

4. Identify one way you can reflect God's message positively to others over the next week. Do it!

5. Identify an issue in our world that concerns you.

6. Review the attitudes which are part of being a man of God in Section IV; identify one attitude you want to demonstrate to others regularly.

7. Psalm 143:10 states: "Teach me to do what you want, because you are my God. May your good Spirit lead me on a level path." How does this Bible verse apply to your manhood journey?

8. As a group, discuss the next step in your pursuit of manhood. Is it important to you to continue your manhood growth process collectively, with a group of men? We invite you to join us, as we all work to become better men of God in SQUIRE: THE TRAINING OF THE KNIGHT.

Answer Key

Lesson 1 - Page 1
I. C. relationship
    D. 3. • gift
III. C. 1. adjusting

Lesson 2 - Page 7
I. A. 1. comfort
    B. 1. US

Lesson 3 - Page 13
B. 1. • character
    7. • (whatever you call it)
       • true

Lesson 4 - Page 20
I. G. Him
III. A. blame

Lesson 5 - Page 27
I. A. 3. filled
II. negatively
III. A. heal

Lesson 6 - Page 34
II. E. realistic
I. follow
III. C. 2. • committed

Our Viewpoint

The Knights of the 21st Century material is written based on several basic life assumptions. Those who participate in this program are encouraged to evaluate their beliefs, and make decisions about their beliefs if they have previously ignored this important area of their lives. They must also become aware of the fact that their beliefs are the basis upon which many of their life choices are made. A basic tenet of the Knights curriculum is that males have great potential if they choose to become men, which makes developing positive expectations of how a man is defined an important key to achieving manhood. Life (or the forest) will throw issue after issue, experience after experience, and numerous types of relationships at the average man on his journey. Males crumble, take detours that waste their time and their lives, dumb themselves down, and choose to get involved in negative activities, all as a result of not knowing the principles of manhood and choosing to live by them. A man, in contrast, takes the time to reflect, and acquire certainty, regarding the foundational elements of his beliefs. The man learns, as the weight of the world crushes in on him, to utilize the depth of this basic understanding of his beliefs to assist him and to choose the manhood journey. The 15 Principles of Manhood[‡] have been offered as a starting place for the manhood journey, but it is recommended that principles of a more personal nature be developed by each man. The foundational thinking of the Knights curriculum can be understood further by the following assumptions upon which this material is based. It is hoped that these thoughts will stimulate your thinking regarding the ideas that are an essential part of your manhood journey.

Assumption 1: The world has many seemingly unsolvable problems that encourage deteriorating relationships, aggression, and an abundance of negative news coverage. These problems are a result of the choices of many of the male gender who refuse to give up their simplistic boyish ways and choose to ignore their manhood calling.

Assumption 2: Men who choose to follow the arduous path that is required for the achievement of their manhood potential are, in reality, all heroes. They have accepted their calling and developed the strengths that are needed to be successful, as men. It is only through such heroic efforts and wise choices that a man does not choose the easier route by staying a boy. The man who chooses to exercise himself to grow toward manhood can become the man that this world needs. Heroic men can make a difference in the lives of others and in the forest.

Assumption 3: At Knights of the 21st Century, we believe that one of the best explanations of human life, as we understand it, is described in the Bible. The Biblical faith choice allows a person to recognize the problems that are associated with the very foundations of human experience, and at the same time, provide a man with hopeful and adequate solutions. As a result of human choice, the Bible teaches that man has left God's original design, making the world chaotic, which contributes to negative experiences for all. Instead of government or corporate solutions, the Bible teaches that the world must be changed by one valuable human life at a time, each one choosing to turn over the direction of their ongoing existence to God's loving purpose for them. This is how to change the world!

Assumption 4: In the Bible, God tells us that the only way to have an ongoing relationship with Him is through a spiritual rebirth experience. This occurs when a man accepts Christ's death on the cross, which is the only way to spiritually deal with his imperfect choices. Man's sin (or shadow) not only harms him, it also violates the attributes of holiness and justice that are part of who God is. Christ is the ultimate example of manhood; He fulfilled His potential; He sacrificed Himself for the good of others; He demonstrated His strength as He walked through the challenges of life.

Assumption 5: You must choose whether you want a relationship with God. The nature of this choice means that there are other belief alternatives in the world. God loves each person in the world; He gives them great potential, and the ability to choose or reject Him. The Knights material is written in a way that respects your choice not to believe in God, while also attempting to be Biblically consistent with those who choose to believe. It is our belief that all of life is a result of God's original gift; human potential is not an exception to God's grace.

A man's faith choices may change as a result of following the Knights of the 21st Century concepts and principles and learning to think more deeply about life. We attempt to honor our Hero, Jesus Christ, by helping males, who are not yet heroes, take advantage of God's gift by building up their manhood potential, helping the world change for good, and feeling Christ's love for them. As a result of the diversity of the faith systems of the men taking this manhood course and the author's belief that all truth is God's truth, some people will be quoted who may differ individually from the author's Biblical viewpoint. Truth, when expressed by someone with a different faith system, cannot differ from God's truth; it is used to understand the world and to deal nobly with its challenges.

‡ Visit **http://bit.ly/principlesofmanhood** or **http://bit.ly/1ueLjr7** to view the images we have associated with the 15 Principles of Manhood.

Our Team

Author: Dr. Roy Smith...has worked for over 30 years as a psychologist/counselor to men and their families. He developed the Knights of the 21ˢᵗ Century program to help men grow, which helps them learn how to lead more effectively and contributes to the over-reaching goal of positively changing our culture. Roy has a Master's of Divinity degree and a Ph.D. in psychology. He would describe himself as a lucky man because of his marriage to Jan, who is also a therapist, and because of her ongoing support for many of his idealistic "windmill attacks." Roy and Jan have two children, Kim and Nick.

Key Presenter: Keith Walker...serves at Lives Changed By Christ (LCBC) as the lead teacher of the weekly sessions of Knights of the 21ˢᵗ Century.

Director: Ruthie Davis...is a former missionary kid from Thailand, serves in leadership at Pennsylvania Counseling Services, and has a passion for supporting Knights of the 21ˢᵗ Century because of how it is changing men's lives and those of their families.

Director of Team Development: Clair Hoover...has led the Knight's leadership team at LCBC for over eight years. He has been married to his bride, Bonnie, for over 25 years and they are the proud parents of 2 sons, Shane and Cameron.

Editor: Barb Sabo...has worked at PCS for over 20 years. The editing skills that are a "part of her being" belong to her Mom...and it is with love and hope that these skills are shared with all of the men who hope and aim to become knights.

Copy Editor: Trisha Hocker...graduated from Lebanon Valley College with a Bachelor's degree in Business Administration/Management.

Copy Editor: Laura Cramer...is a sophomore at University of Pittsburgh, studying neuroscience.

Production Assistant: Stephanie Faehling...enjoys working on the creative aspects of Knights of the 21ˢᵗ Century and has been the Director of Education at Pennsylvania Counseling Services for over 12 years.

Our Mission

A man always needs a place to meet with other men to talk honestly about himself and life. The pace of daily activities is such that a man can easily make life into a list, himself into a machine to do the list, and the people around him evaluated only in relationship to the list that must be done. Men who gather for fun, a teaching challenge, and a campfire time of sharing, encourage each other to move beyond this style of living. A time for growth, self-reflection, and relationship support helps men to hold each other accountable and fulfill their potential at a higher level by first learning to change and lead themselves. Men who lead themselves in better ways are then able to lead those they love and more positively affect the culture in which they live. Let us commit together, right now, to becoming heroic men who make a difference in the 21st century.

We would appreciate your help in improving the Knights curriculum. Please contact us at feedback@knightsofthe21stcentury.com with any comments, suggestions, tips or ideas that you may have as you attend your men's meetings. In addition, please follow our blog by signing up for a weekly video message at www.manhoodtalk.com.

A Knight's Definition of Manhood

Manhood is an attitude (state), not a once and done achievement (stage). A man actively displays his manly attitude by continuously:

1. Preparing himself for any cultural threats or fights ahead.

2. Developing and strengthening himself, so as to always be at his best.

3. Learning to understand and utilize his complexity as he endeavors to choose wisely and responsibly.

4. Deciding to apply his principles through an orientation toward positive action.

5. Fulfilling his unique calling to help others, so as to reflect God's abiding love for them.

Survey

Instructions: Leaders – Please provide a copy of the survey to each participant. The survey may be downloaded from knights21.com/genesisofmanhoodextras or photocopies of the survey may be made. The participants should complete the survey and return it to you for your review.

Please send copies of the completed surveys to us by any of the following methods:

Scan and email: genesisofmanhood@knights21.com
Fax: 1.717.272.5539
Mail completed surveys: Knights Survey
           200 North Seventh Street
           Lebanon, PA 17046

1. This program has helped me grow (circle all that apply): spiritually, as a man, as a husband, as a father, as a friend **OR** it did not help me grow in any of these areas.

2. I liked my group experience..YES or NO

3. I was able to connect with the men in my group. ....YES or NO

4. I felt I could share honestly with my group about real struggles that I was facing in my personal life. ....YES or NO

   Comments: _____

   _____

   _____

5. Sharing my thoughts and feelings in a group is easy for me to do.
   (Disagree) 1 2 3 4 5 (Agree)

6. I am growing in positive ways in my manhood journey.
   (Disagree) 1 2 3 4 5 (Agree)

7. I would feel comfortable inviting my non-church friends or neighbors to our men's group. ....YES or NO

8. My group demonstrated good listening skills.

(Disagree) 1 2 3 4 5 (Agree)

9. My group showed respect for differing spiritual viewpoints and/ or thoughts and opinions.

(Disagree) 1 2 3 4 5 (Agree)

10. My group leader did a good job running the group......YES or NO

11. My group leader gave each of us equal time to share.....YES or NO

12. Our group leader could improve in the following ways:_____
   _____
   _____

13. I appreciate the Knighthood "Thought for the Day."....YES or NO
    (If you haven't signed up for the Knighthood "Thought for the Day," please visit knights21.com.)

14. Rate your overall *Genesis of Manhood* experience.

(Didn't like) 1 2 3 4 5 (Great)

Comments: _____
   _____

15. I would like our group to start the Knights curriculum –
    Squire: The Training of the Knight. ....YES or NO

16. I would like to stay with my group. ....YES or NO

17. I would like to be assigned to a new group. ....YES or NO

18. If needed, I would be willing to be a group leader.......YES or NO

A Consideration

We are aware that the men taking this course may each be in different phases of the manhood journey. There will be men who have never married and men who are widowed or divorced. The diversity of the situations to which the Knights resources can be applied is endless; every effort has been made to reach out to all individuals, at whatever point of growth they may be in their manhood journey. As some men apply the concepts of being a knight to their relationships with their wife or child(ren), others may be learning to be a knight to someone they are dating or to a friend. All of these men are needed for the forest-changing men's movement that lies ahead, because heroes come from all walks of life. Men who participate in the Knights program will vary in their faith structure, educational status, and cultural heritage. Men who are in prisons, or who participate in weekend retreats, or in church and business settings can all work to strengthen themselves using the Knights of the 21st Century curriculum. Because the underlying concepts of the Knights curriculum can push the upper limits of some men's learning capacity, permission should be given for each man to work at his own pace in ways that make it easy for him to apply it to his life. Please adjust the lesson or the questions, if needed, to make it more relevant to you and your group. Feel free to share any changes you make to the Knights curriculum materials through the various feedback options (i.e., the survey found in this book or send an email to **genesisofmanhood@knights21.com**). Thank you for your consideration.

WHAT YOU DO ONLINE
IMPACTS YOUR LIFE OFFLINE

TRY COVENANT EYES FREE
FOR 30 DAYS USING THIS
PROMO CODE: **knights**

Guard yourself and your
loved ones with Internet
Accountability and Filtering.

ACCOUNTABILITY SOFTWARE

- ✓ Monitors and reports Internet use
- ✓ Each site is rated (such as T for Teen, M for Mature, etc.)
- ✓ Reports are sent to a person you choose: a parent, friend, or mentor.
- ✓ Use Reports to have conversations about online temptations.
- ✓ Available for Windows and Mac computers, iPhone®, iPad®, iPod touch®, Android™ phones and tablets.

FILTERING SOFTWARE

- ✓ Blocks inappropriate content.
- ✓ Customizable block/allow lists.
- ✓ Choose the times of day the web may be accessed. (Not available for mobile.)
- ✓ Available for Windows, Mac, iPhone, iPad, and iPod touch.

Find Covenant Eyes on:

📍 1525 W. King St., PO Box 637
Owosso, MI 48867 ☎ Toll free in US 877.479.1119 💻 www.covenanteyes.com

ADDITIONAL KNIGHTS OF THE 21ST CENTURY PRODUCTS

For more products, visit our website store at Knights21.com.

MANHOOD JOURNEY

A man is designed for a special Godly purpose, for which God has given him great potential. Knights of the 21st Century, a men's ministry curriculum used by churches around the world, is based on the material in this book, and serves as the foundation for many of the Knights resource materials.

BULL

Every male has the drive to become a real man. Other men guide him on this adventure. A strong father invests in his son's manhood quest. This book challenges courageous warriors on their God-intended journey.

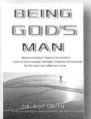

BEING GOD'S MAN

This book explores what it means to be God's man and to reflect Jesus Christ to others on a daily basis. A man's ability to reflect Jesus to others requires him to integrate God into all of who he is.

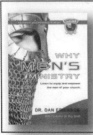

WHY MEN'S MINISTRY

A strong men's ministry is foundational to the church's fulfillment of God's great purpose for the world. This book discusses the issues that are important to an effective men's ministry program and empowers leaders to provide the kind of program that changes men's lives.